OUT OF THIS WORLD

STARGAZING

ALEX KUSKOWSKI

Consulting Editor, Diane Craig, M.A./Reading Specialist

Super Sandcastle

An Imprint of Abdo Publishing
abdopublishing.com

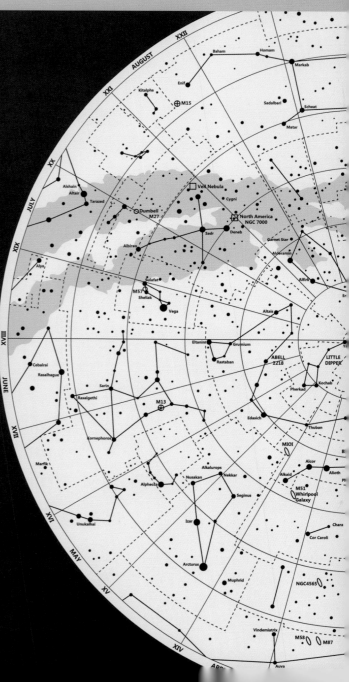

ABDOPUBLISHING.COM

Published by Abdo Publishing, a division of ABDO, PO Box 398166, Minneapolis, Minnesota 55439. Copyright © 2016 by Abdo Consulting Group, Inc. International copyrights reserved in all countries. No part of this book may be reproduced in any form without written permission from the publisher. Super SandCastle™ is a trademark and logo of Abdo Publishing.

Printed in the United States of America, North Mankato, Minnesota
062015
092015

Editor: Liz Salzmann
Content Developer: Nancy Tuminelly
Cover and Interior Design and Production: Mighty Media, Inc.
Photo Credits: NASA, Shutterstock

Library of Congress Cataloging-in-Publication Data
Kuskowski, Alex, author.
  Stargazing / Alex Kuskowski ; consulting editor, Diane Craig, M.A./Reading Specialist.
      pages cm. -- (Out of this world)
  Audience: K to grade 4
  ISBN 978-1-62403-746-7
  1. Stars--Juvenile literature. 2. Constellations--Juvenile literature. 3. Telescopes--Juvenile literature. I. Title.
  QB46.K87 2016
  523.8--dc23
                      2015002211

Super SandCastle™ books are created by a team of professional educators, reading specialists, and content developers around five essential components—phonemic awareness, phonics, vocabulary, text comprehension, and fluency—to assist young readers as they develop reading skills and strategies and increase their general knowledge. All books are written, reviewed, and leveled for guided reading, early reading intervention, and Accelerated Reader™ programs for use in shared, guided, and independent reading and writing activities to support a balanced approach to literacy instruction.

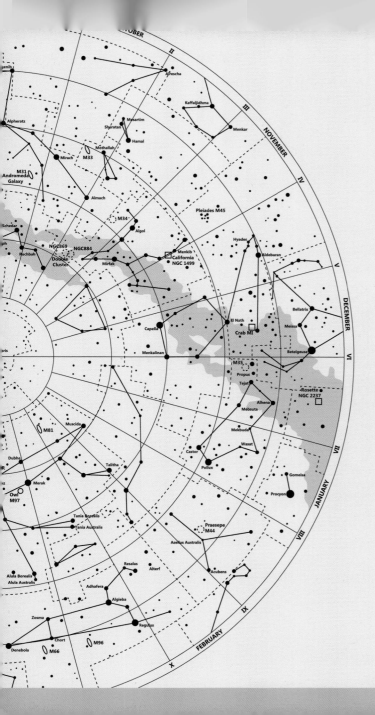

CONTENTS

4	Secrets of the Sky
5	What Is a Star?
6	Starry Sky
8	Constellations
10	Mapping the Night
12	Astronomers
14	The Telescope
16	Super Scopes
18	The Sky Is Falling
20	Astronomy Now
22	Try It Out!
23	Become a Stargazer
23	Stargazing Quiz
24	Glossary

SECRETS OF THE SKY

Look up at night! What's out there? Explore the oldest science, astronomy. It is the study of the objects in space. That includes stars, meteors, and planets.

METEOR

A small rock that hits Earth's atmosphere. It burns up, creating a bright **streak**.

STARS

On a clear night, your eyes can see thousands of stars!

PLANET

A large object in space that orbits a star.

WHAT IS A STAR?

STARS ARE MADE OF VERY HOT GASES

A **STAR** is a huge, shining **sphere**. It is held together by its own gravity. The sun is Earth's nearest star.

STARS GROW AND CHANGE OVER MILLIONS OF YEARS

TIME ⟶

STARRY SKY

Starlight takes a very long time to reach Earth. The light we see is millions of years old!

HOT AND COLD

Stars come in many colors. The temperature of the star **determines** its color.

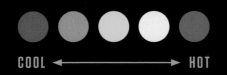

COOL ⟷ HOT

Hot stars are white or blue. Cool stars are orange or red.

COOL STARS

HOT STARS

ROUND AND ROUND THE EARTH

The Earth spins. It gives us day and night. The night sky moves from east to west, just like the sun!

During the night, some stars appear in the east. They disappear in the west.

Some stars don't seem to move. Those stars are near the north and south poles.

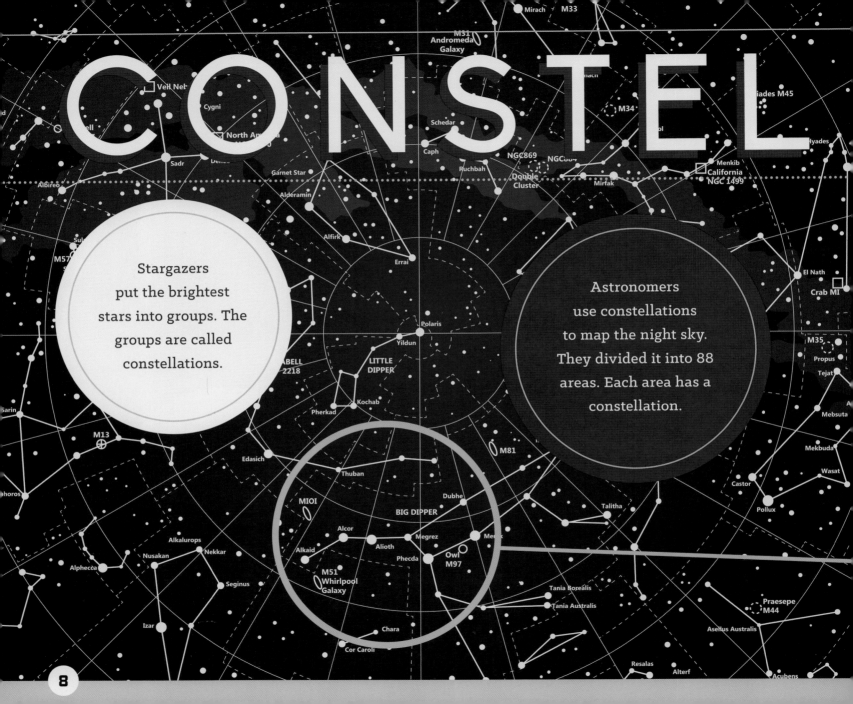

CONSTEL

Stargazers put the brightest stars into groups. The groups are called constellations.

Astronomers use constellations to map the night sky. They divided it into 88 areas. Each area has a constellation.

Imaginary lines join the stars. They make a picture.

A BEAR IN THE SKY

The constellation Ursa Major is easy to spot. Ursa Major means Great Bear. The seven brightest stars in Ursa Major are called the Big Dipper.

MAPPING THE NIGHT

PEOPLE REALIZED that the stars stayed in the same patterns. So they mapped them out. Constellations helped people remember the map. Some star maps are thousands of years old!

SAILING STAR CHARTS

Before star maps, sailors stayed near the coasts. Mapping the stars changed sailing. People went all over the world.

THE NORTHERN SKY

NORTH OR SOUTH

The night sky looks different from different parts of Earth. Some stars can only be seen above the equator. Some stars can only be seen below the equator!

THE SOUTHERN SKY

POLARIS

Polaris is a star that never moves. It always is in the north. It is also called the North Star. People can use it to find their way!

POLARIS

ASTRONOMERS

NICOLAUS COPERNICUS (1473–1543)

Copernicus was the first one to say the Earth was not the center of the universe. Many people did not believe him.

GALILEO GALILEI (1564–1642)

Galileo got into trouble for his stargazing. He argued that everything orbited the sun. He improved the telescope too!

PEOPLE WHO STUDY THE NIGHT SKY ARE CALLED ASTRONOMERS. ASTRONOMERS MAKE DISCOVERIES THAT CHANGE THE WORLD.

ANNIE CANNON (1863–1941)

Cannon created a method of **classifying** stars. She classified more than 250,000 stars. She also discovered 300 new stars.

ALBERT EINSTEIN (1879–1955)

Einstein found a new way to look at the universe. He made many discoveries. He used math to show that the sun could bend light!

THE TELESCOPE

LIGHT

LENS

Light enters a large glass lens.

Telescopes help people see objects in the night sky.

THE BIGGER THE LENS IS, THE MORE YOU CAN SEE!

A MODERN TELESCOPE

TELESCOPES FOCUS LIGHT FROM FARAWAY OBJECTS, SUCH AS STARS AND PLANETS. THEY ARE EASIER TO SEE.

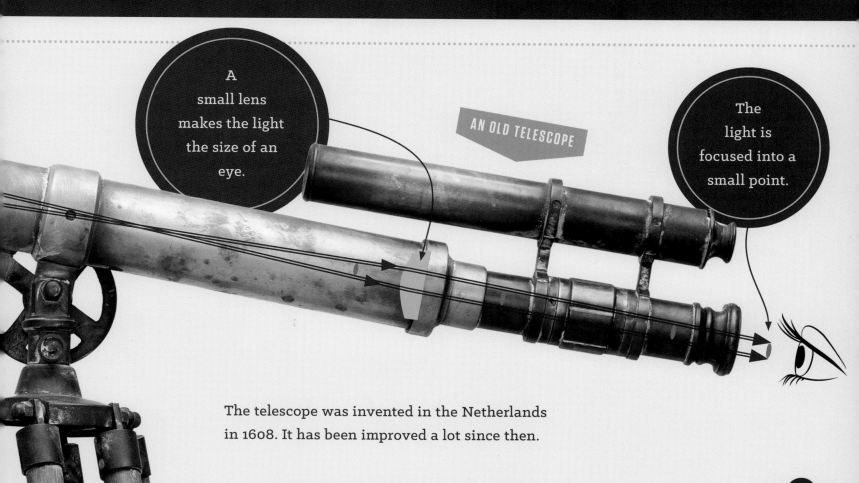

A small lens makes the light the size of an eye.

AN OLD TELESCOPE

The light is focused into a small point.

The telescope was invented in the Netherlands in 1608. It has been improved a lot since then.

SUPER SCOPES

Astronomers use giant telescopes. They are built on mountaintops away from cities. It makes the sky easier to see.

OBSERVATORIES

An observatory has a giant telescope inside a **dome**. The top of the dome turns. The telescope can look at different parts of the sky.

DIFFERENT SCOPES FOR DIFFERENT FOLKS

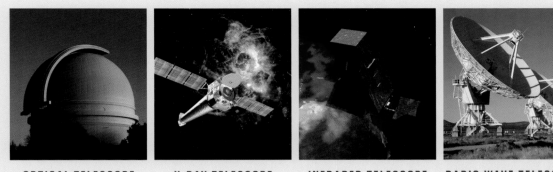

OPTICAL TELESCOPE

X-RAY TELESCOPE

INFRARED TELESCOPE

RADIO WAVE TELESCOPE

SCOPES IN SPACE

The Hubble Telescope is a telescope in space! Astronomers can control and use it from Earth.

THE SKY IS FALLING

SHOOTING STARS

Sometimes it looks like a star is falling. People call it a shooting star. But it isn't really a star at all. It is a meteor.

A meteor is a rock that hits Earth's atmosphere. It burns up, which creates a **streak** of light.

METEOR SHOWER

A meteor shower can sometimes be seen at night. Many meteors can burn up at the same time. It looks like a lot of shooting stars!

MIGHTY METEORITES

Sometimes a meteor doesn't burn up completely. It falls to the ground. Then it is called a meteorite. Scientists study meteorites to learn more about outer space.

IMPACT CRATERS

Most meteorites are small. But sometimes a big meteorite falls to Earth. It can make a hole when it hits. It is called an **impact** crater.

COMETS

A comet is a frozen ball of rock, ice, and gases. Heat from the sun causes dust and gas to stream behind it.

ASTRONOMY

Astronomers study all of space. Some look at planets. Some look at the sun. Some look at faraway stars.

PLANETARY ASTRONOMERS

Planetary astronomers study planets, moons, comets, and asteroids in our solar system.

NOW

SOLAR ASTRONOMERS

The most studied star is the closest one, our sun. Many astronomers study the sun. They use it to learn more about other stars.

STELLAR ASTRONOMERS

Studying faraway stars is important. **Stellar** astronomers think it could explain the whole universe.

TRY IT OUT!

Astronomy is something you can do from home! Regular people help astronomers make **amazing** finds.

CITIZEN SCIENTISTS are indoor astronomers. They look over pictures from telescopes. They find planets.

AMATEUR ASTRONOMERS watch the night sky. They use their eyes, **binoculars**, and telescopes. They discover comets and asteroids.

STARGAZING QUIZ

1.   What star is known as the North Star and never moves?

2.   What colors can hot stars be?

3.   Planetary astronomers study faraway stars. *True or false?*

THINK ABOUT IT!

What kind of astronomer would you want to be and why?

Answers 1. Polaris   2. White or blue   3. False

GLOSSARY

amateur – someone who does something for pleasure, not money.

amazing – wonderful or surprising.

binoculars – a magnifying device you look through with both eyes to get a better look at things that are far away.

classify – to put things in groups according to their characteristics.

determine – to cause an outcome or have an affect on something.

dome – a roof shaped like half of a sphere.

impact – when something hits something else very hard.

sphere – a figure that is round, such as a ball or a globe.

stellar – related to the stars.

streak – a long, thin mark or stripe.